THE MINDFUL CONSCIOUS LEADER

MEDITATION TECHNIQUES FOR MODERN MANAGEMENT

DR. MINAKSHI BANSAL

Contents

Contents

Prayer

"Om Bhadram Karnebhih Shrinuyama Devah
Bhadram Pashyemakshabhiryajatrah
Sthirairangais Tushtuvamsastanubhih
Vyashema Devahitam Yadayuh
Svasti Na Indro Vriddhashravah
Svasti Nah Pusha Vishwavedah
Svasti Nastarkshyo Arishtanemih
Svasti No Brihaspatir Dadhatu
Om Shantih Shantih Shantih"

This mantra is a prayer for universal well-being, invoking the blessings of various deities for protection, health, and happiness. It emphasizes the importance of experiencing the auspicious through all senses and living a life aligned with divine purpose. The repetition of "Shantih" at the end signifies a deep desire for peace in the individual, the environment, and the universe at large. This mantra is often recited as a prayer for peace, prosperity, and the physical and spiritual well-being of all beings.

▷▷▷

About The Author

Dr. Minakshi Bansal, born in the bustling metropolis of Delhi, India, has led a life steeped in artistry, scholarly pursuit, and an unwavering commitment to societal betterment. Following her marriage, she relocated to Ahmedabad, Gujarat, where she has since blossomed into a multifaceted beacon of inspiration for many. Dr. Minakshi is not only recognized as a gifted artist in the realm of Fine Arts but also as an esteemed author, a devoted social worker and a dedicated research scholar in Psychology. Her journey, marked by a profound dedication to elevating those around her, especially the downtrodden and underprivileged children of society, is a testament to her deep-seated belief in the transformative power of engagement and empathy.

From her earliest days, Minakshi was distinguished by an insatiable appetite for reading. Her literary universe was inhabited by characters and narratives that spanned ethical tales, motivational and inspirational stories, and the mythic parables imbued with life lessons. This voracious reading habit was not merely for personal edification but was driven by a desire to distill and disseminate the essence of these narratives to foster the development of students and peers alike. She was particularly captivated by the lives and teachings of historical figures and spiritual leaders such as Adi Shankaracharya, Swami Vivekananda, Dr. APJ Abdul Kalam, Mahamana Pandit Madan Mohan Malviya, Mahatma Gandhi, Sardar Vallabhai Patel, and Vinoba Bhave, among others. Their philosophies and life stories fueled her ambition to embody their ideals of resilience, selflessness, and relentless pursuit of knowledge.

Dr. Minakshi's academic and practical engagement with psychology has been equally noteworthy. As a research scholar, her focus has been on exploring the intricate tapestry of the human

"

psyche, aiming to unlock the potential for psychological well-being and societal harmony. Her scholarly work is complemented by her active involvement in social work, where she employs her academic insights to make tangible differences in the lives of the underprivileged. Her endeavours in social work are characterized by an innovative approach that combines traditional wisdom with contemporary psychological practices to address the multifaceted challenges faced by these communities.

Her artistic talents, another facet of her diverse capabilities, are not merely a personal passion but also serve as a medium through which she communicates and connects with others. Her art, rich in symbolism and emotional depth, reflects her philosophical inquiries and social concerns, offering viewers a glimpse into the breadth of her intellect and the depth of her compassion.

In addition to her contributions to the arts and social sciences, Dr. Minakshi has embraced the healing arts of Pranic Healing, mastering the techniques developed by Master Choa Kok Sui. This practice, which focuses on the manipulation of Prana or life energy to heal the body and aura, has been both a personal journey of discovery and a means through which she extends her healing touch to others. Her proficiency in Pranic Healing is complemented by her advocacy and teaching of various forms of meditation aimed at rejuvenation, personal betterment, and the cultivation of harmony within individuals and communities alike.

Dr. Minakshi's life is a narrative of relentless pursuit, not just of personal achievement but of the upliftment and empowerment of society at large. Her diverse interests and talents—spanning the arts, literature, psychology, and the healing practices—converge on a singular path of service. She embodies the spirit of the luminaries who inspired her, channelling their legacy through her actions and teachings. Through her books, art, and social initiatives, she continues to inspire a new generation to embark on their own journeys of self-discovery, resilience, and altruism.

Her commitment to social betterment, particularly her focus on uplifting underprivileged children, reflects a deep understanding of the transformative potential of education and personal development. By integrating her knowledge of psychology, her artistic sensibilities, and her healing practices, Dr. Bansal has developed a holistic approach to social work that addresses both the immediate needs and the long-term well-being of the communities she serves.

As an author, Dr. Minakshi's writings offer a blend of inspirational insights, practical wisdom, and reflective contemplations drawn from her extensive reading and life experiences. Her books serve as a guide for those seeking to navigate the complexities of life with grace, resilience, and purpose. Through her narratives, she extends an invitation to her readers to explore the depths of their own potential and to contribute meaningfully to the collective well-being of society.

In Dr. Minakshi Bansal, we find a remarkable synthesis of the artist, the scholar, the healer, and the social activist. Her life's work stands as a beacon of hope and a source of inspiration for individuals seeking to make a difference in the world. Her story is a compelling reminder of the power of individual action, rooted in compassion and driven by a profound commitment to the betterment of humanity. Dr. Minakshi's legacy is not just in the tangible outcomes of her efforts but in the enduring spirit of inquiry, empathy, and service that she embodies.

ฅฅฅ

Preface

In the bustling corridors of modern leadership, where the demands are high and the stakes even higher, the quest for innovative management strategies that blend efficacy with personal well-being is ever-present. The impetus to pen this book came from a confluence of personal experiences and professional interactions that illuminated the profound impact of mindfulness on leadership effectiveness. The journey through the pages that follow is one that delves deeply into how the ancient practice of meditation, adapted to the nuances of modern management, can transform the very heart of leadership.

Leadership today is not merely about making decisions or directing teams towards strategic goals. It is increasingly about fostering environments where creativity, resilience, and collaboration can flourish amidst the complexities of global business landscapes. Observing the challenges faced by contemporaries and reflecting on my own experiences in various leadership roles, I was drawn repeatedly to the tranquility and clarity that mindfulness meditation offered. This practice became my steadfast companion, steering me through tumultuous times and guiding me in moments of decision-making.

The narrative of this book is shaped by a simple yet powerful realization: leaders who cultivate mindfulness not only enhance their own lives but also wield the capability to transform their organizations in ways that resonate well beyond the bottom line. Mindfulness in leadership transcends the conventional metrics of success, introducing a spectrum of benefits that include improved mental clarity, enhanced emotional intelligence, and a more profound connection with team members.

This exploration began as a personal quest to understand the intersect between mindfulness and effective leadership. Over time, through discussions with mentors, peers, and experts in the fields of psychology, business, and mindfulness, a richer understanding emerged. These conversations revealed that while many leaders intuitively understand the importance of being present and centered, the pathway to integrating this into their leadership style was less clear.

Structured around practical insights and enriched with real-life examples, this book aims to demystify how meditation can be a powerful tool for leaders. Each chapter meticulously stitches together the theory and practice of mindfulness, tailored specifically for those at the helm of organizations. From fostering emotional resilience to enhancing decision-making and from managing stress to building mindful teams, the scope of this book is broad yet deeply focused on actionable strategies.

The process of writing this book was in itself a reflective practice, where each word and sentence was measured against the backdrop of personal practice and research. The goal was not only to share knowledge but to invite leaders into a dialogue with themselves about the kind of leaders they aspire to be. It is my belief that through such introspection and practice, leadership can be redefined in terms of its capacity to nurture well-being and drive success simultaneously.

Moreover, the principles discussed herein are supported by scientific research that underscores the benefits of mindfulness. Neuroscience and cognitive psychology offer fascinating insights into how mindfulness alters brain patterns, enhancing areas linked to emotional regulation and rational thinking. These scientific underpinnings provide a solid foundation for the practical advice offered, bridging the gap between the mystical perceptions of meditation and its real-world applicability in the demanding arena of leadership.

It is important to note that while the journey into mindful leadership can be profoundly transformative, it is also marked by simplicity. The techniques and strategies laid out in this book do not call for drastic changes in daily routines. Instead, they integrate seamlessly into the existing fabric of daily leadership tasks, requiring nothing more than a commitment to being present and an openness to self-exploration.

This book is for every leader who has ever felt overwhelmed by the pace and pressure of the corporate world, every manager who seeks to lead with compassion and effectiveness, and every individual at the helm of an organization who believes that the path to true leadership excellence weaves through the heart and mind. It is my sincere hope that the pages that follow will not only provide valuable insights but also inspire a commitment to embracing mindfulness as a vital component of effective leadership.

As you embark on this journey through the book, may you find practical wisdom to apply in your leadership practices and may the narrative ignite a transformation that enriches both your professional and personal life. Here's to leading mindfully, leading effectively, and above all, leading with a renewed sense of purpose and well-being.

ԲԲԲ

ONE

INTRODUCTION TO MINDFULNESS IN LEADERSHIP

Mindfulness has emerged as a pivotal element in contemporary leadership, transcending its traditional roots in spiritual and therapeutic realms to become a fundamental skill in the toolkit of modern managers. As the pace of business accelerates and the complexity of workplace challenges grows, leaders across various industries are turning to mindfulness to steer their teams with greater competence and calm. The essence of mindfulness in leadership lies in its ability to foster a deep, clear presence that enhances decision-making, communication, and conflict resolution.

At its core, mindfulness involves maintaining a moment-by-moment awareness of our thoughts, feelings, bodily sensations, and the surrounding environment. This practice typically involves a high degree of acceptance — meaning that we pay attention to our thoughts and feelings without judging them as good or bad. Instead of letting life pass by, mindfulness means living in the moment and awakening to experience. When applied to leadership, this translates into a management style that is reflective rather than reactive, informed by a thorough understanding of one's mental and emotional landscape.

The importance of mindfulness in modern management cannot be overstated. In an era where leaders are expected to navigate constantly changing business landscapes, the calm and focus afforded by mindfulness are invaluable. Leaders who practice mindfulness are better equipped to respond to stress and adversity with poise, preserving their own well-being and setting a powerful example for their teams. Moreover, mindfulness enhances emotional intelligence, a key attribute in effective leadership, by improving the ability to understand, empathize, and connect with others.

Mindful leadership also contributes to improved workplace dynamics. By encouraging a mindful approach, leaders can create a more positive and productive work environment. For instance, mindfulness helps leaders to recognize their biases and avoid reactive emotional responses. This capability is crucial in managing diverse teams, as it promotes inclusiveness and helps prevent conflicts from escalating. Additionally, when leaders handle stress better, it reduces the overall tension within the team, leading to increased satisfaction and reduced turnover.

Furthermore, the practice of mindfulness aids in developing several competencies essential for leadership success. One of the most significant is enhanced decision-making. With mindfulness, leaders can clear their minds of clutter, focus on the present, and derive insights from a balanced and comprehensive viewpoint. This ability to concentrate deeply on the issue at hand without distraction leads to better, more thoughtful decisions. Another competency is the enhancement of creativity and innovation. Mindfulness practices such as meditation can relax the mind and foster an open state where new ideas can surface. In today's fast-paced business world, where innovation is often a key to staying ahead, such an advantage is invaluable.

Moreover, the adoption of mindfulness in leadership goes beyond individual benefits, influencing the broader organizational culture. Leaders who practice mindfulness set a tone that emphasizes thoughtful interaction and reflective thinking. This cultural shift can lead to greater levels of engagement and collaboration as employees mimic these behaviors in their interactions. By embedding mindfulness into the organizational ethos, leaders can help cultivate a more supportive, resilient workforce prepared to meet future challenges with confidence and creativity.

Despite these advantages, integrating mindfulness into leadership practices is not without challenges. It requires a commitment to ongoing practice and a willingness to look inward and confront uncomfortable truths about oneself. However, for those leaders who commit to the journey, the rewards can be profound, not only for themselves but also for the organizations they lead. As businesses continue to operate in an increasingly complex and unpredictable world, the principles of mindfulness offer a beacon of stability and clarity.

In sum, mindfulness is not just a personal practice but a critical component of modern management that can significantly enhance leadership effectiveness. By fostering greater awareness, emotional intelligence, and a calm, centered approach to challenges, mindful leaders can inspire and lead their teams to achieve exceptional results. As we look to the future of leadership, the integration of mindfulness into daily leadership practices stands as a promising path toward developing more adaptable, compassionate, and effective leaders.

ppp

"Mindful leadership begins with self-awareness; it
is about understanding your own emotions before
you can effectively lead others. It's the quiet yet
profound journey of discovering your potential to
influence with compassion and clarity."

ᐳᐳᐳ

TWO

HE MINDFUL LEADER'S MORNING

The morning sets the tone for the day, especially for leaders whose schedules are typically packed and whose decisions impact entire organizations. For a leader embracing mindfulness, the morning is not just the start of the workday but a sacred space for grounding and preparing oneself to face the myriad challenges that lie ahead with clarity and purpose. This ritual, when practiced with intention, can significantly influence a leader's effectiveness throughout the day, enhancing their ability to manage themselves and their teams.

The Foundation of a Mindful Morning

Establishing a mindful morning routine begins the night before. A leader's ability to wake up feeling refreshed and ready to engage mindfully with their day often hinges on the quality of their sleep. Thus, mindfulness actually starts with ensuring a proper wind-down routine in the evening, which might include dimming the lights, turning off electronic devices an hour before bed, and engaging in calming activities such as reading or meditation. These practices not only improve sleep quality but also help in transitioning from the day's stresses, setting the stage for a morning that begins on a positive note.

Upon waking, instead of diving straight into emails or the day's news, mindful leaders can benefit from instituting a 'digital pause'—deliberately delaying the use of any digital devices. This practice shields one's early hours from external pressures and distractions, allowing the leader to anchor themselves in their intentions for the day without the influence of external noise.

Mindful Practices to Start the Day

Meditation: One of the most effective techniques for starting the day with clarity and purpose is meditation. A brief session, even just five to ten minutes, can immensely enhance a leader's focus and stress management capabilities. Meditation practices might vary from focused attention on the breath, body scans to recognize and release any physical tension, or visualization techniques to imagine the successful outcomes of the day's tasks. This not only clears the mind but also equips leaders with enhanced patience and mindfulness as they proceed through their schedule.

Journaling: Another powerful tool in the mindful leader's morning arsenal is journaling. Spending a few minutes each morning to jot down thoughts, intentions, and goals can provide a clear roadmap for the day. It helps in prioritizing tasks and aligning them with broader objectives, ensuring that daily activities contribute to long-term goals. Moreover, journaling can be a reflective practice, helping leaders to track their progress, understand their emotional states over time, and gain insights into their leadership styles and personal growth.

Mindful Movement: Physical exercise, integrated with mindfulness, can be particularly beneficial in the morning.

Whether it is yoga, a gentle stretch routine, or a more vigorous workout, the key is to remain fully present and connected with the body during the activity. This practice not only energizes the body and prepares it for the physical demands of the day but also sharpens mental acuity and emotional resilience.

Mindful Eating: Breakfast is often overlooked in a rush to start the workday, but it is an essential element of a mindful morning. A calm, focused meal where a leader pays attention to the taste, texture, and nourishment of their food can set a precedent for mindful choices throughout the day. It also serves as a reminder that food is fuel and that the body's needs must not be neglected amidst professional responsibilities.

Setting Intentions for the Day

Before the workday officially begins, setting intentions can immensely benefit mindful leaders. This practice involves taking a few moments to define what they wish to achieve and how they intend to behave throughout the day. Intentions might be specific, like resolving a particular issue, or more general, such as maintaining a positive attitude or being open to new ideas. This clear definition of one's goals not only provides a focused path for the day's efforts but also helps in aligning the team's efforts when shared or communicated effectively.

Mindful leadership in the morning isn't just about individual practices; it's about setting a pattern of behavior that permeates throughout the organization. When leaders demonstrate commitment to their well-being and purpose right from the start of the day, they inspire their teams to adopt similar practices. This can lead to a workplace culture that values clarity, purpose, and well-being, which are essential for sustaining performance and ensuring a healthy work environment.

Thus, a mindful leader's morning is a cornerstone of effective leadership. By establishing and adhering to a morning routine that emphasizes mindfulness, leaders can not only enhance their own daily performance but also foster an environment where mindfulness is valued and practiced at all levels. This alignment between personal practice and organizational culture is what ultimately drives sustained success and well-being in the workplace.

᠀᠀᠀

"In the realm of effective leadership, the power of mindfulness lies not in the silence of meditation alone but in its application in daily decisions and interactions. True leadership strength flows from a calm and centered mind."

▷▷▷

THREE

CULTIVATING PRESENCE

Cultivating presence is a fundamental aspect of mindfulness, particularly for leaders in a corporate environment where the pace can be frenetic and the distractions numerous. Presence, or the ability to remain fully aware and engaged in the current moment, is crucial for effective leadership. It enhances the quality of interactions, decision-making, and the leader's ability to respond to challenges and opportunities with a clear mind and a focused approach.

The Significance of Presence in Leadership

Presence is more than just physical attendance in meetings or conversations; it involves an attentive and conscious connection with the current situation and the individuals involved. For leaders, being present means actively listening, observing, and participating in interactions without preconceived notions or distractions. This level of engagement is vital as it influences how leaders are perceived by their teams and how effectively they can motivate and inspire those around them.

The ability to be present also allows leaders to better manage their emotions and reactions. When fully engaged, a leader can sense emerging conflicts or misunderstandings and address them proactively. Similarly, presence can enhance the perception of empathy, a critical leadership trait, as it involves understanding and responding to the emotions and needs of others.

Practices to Enhance Presence

Mindfulness Meditation: Regular mindfulness meditation is one of the most effective ways to enhance presence. This practice involves focusing on the breath or a mantra, guiding the mind away from distracting thoughts and toward a state of centered awareness. Even a few minutes a day can help improve a leader's ability to remain present during stressful situations. Over time, this practice not only helps in reducing stress but also improves cognitive functions related to attention and regulation of emotions.

Active Listening: Active listening is a crucial skill for cultivating presence. It requires leaders to fully concentrate, understand, respond, and then remember what is being said. Techniques include maintaining eye contact, nodding, and paraphrasing what others have said to confirm understanding. This not only helps in building trust and rapport but also ensures that leaders do not miss critical nuances in communication.

Single-Tasking: In a world that often values multitasking, single-tasking can be a powerful method for enhancing presence. This involves committing to one task at a time and giving it full attention until completion. For leaders, this might mean scheduling blocks of time for different tasks, including periods solely for strategic thinking or employee interaction, without the interference of phone calls or emails.

Mindful Pauses: Integrating brief mindful pauses throughout the day is another effective way to cultivate presence. These are short periods, perhaps only a minute or two, where leaders can stop their current activity, take deep breaths, and re-center their focus. These pauses can be especially useful before transitioning between different types of tasks or before entering meetings.

Reflective Practice: Reflective practice involves taking time at the end of the day or after key events to reflect on what occurred, how it was handled, and how it could be improved. This practice can help leaders become more aware of their habitual patterns of thought and behavior, which in turn enhances their ability to remain present and engaged.

Technology Hygiene: Managing technology use is essential for cultivating presence. Leaders should set boundaries on their use of devices, especially during critical interactions or when needing to focus deeply. Techniques can include designated times to check emails, turning off notifications during meetings, or even implementing device-free zones in the office.

Applying Presence in Daily Interactions

The real test of a leader's ability to cultivate presence lies in their daily interactions. Whether it's a formal meeting, a casual conversation, or even an email exchange, each touchpoint offers an opportunity to practice presence. By consistently applying the practices of mindfulness, active listening, and single-tasking, leaders not only improve their own effectiveness but also foster a more attentive and engaged organizational culture.

Ultimately, the benefits of cultivating presence extend beyond the immediate gains in communication and decision-making. They contribute to a more compassionate, responsive, and adaptive leadership style, laying the foundation for a workplace that values and practices mindfulness at every level. As leaders become more present, they inspire their teams to adopt similar behaviors, leading to a collective increase in productivity, well-being, and satisfaction across the organization. This culture of presence can become a significant competitive advantage, enabling the organization to navigate the complexities of the modern business environment with agility and grace.

ᗏᗏᗏ

"Cultivating a culture of mindfulness within an organization doesn't just enhance well-being; it fosters a foundation of trust and creativity that can weather any storm. Every mindful moment counts."

ᐅᐅᐅ

FOUR

EMOTIONAL INTELLIGENCE THROUGH MINDFULNESS

Emotional intelligence (EI) has emerged as a key factor in effective leadership, distinguishing exceptional leaders from their peers. It refers to the ability to understand, use, and manage one's own emotions in positive ways to relieve stress, communicate effectively, empathize with others, overcome challenges, and defuse conflict. Integrating mindfulness into the cultivation of emotional intelligence can greatly enhance a leader's capacity for emotional resilience and responsiveness, enabling them to lead more effectively and foster a positive workplace culture.

Understanding Emotional Intelligence in Leadership

At its core, emotional intelligence in leadership involves four main components: self-awareness, self-management, social awareness, and relationship management. Each component plays a crucial role in a leader's ability to function and interact within the complexities of organizational dynamics.

Self-awareness involves recognizing one's own emotions and how they affect thoughts and behavior. This awareness allows leaders to understand their strengths and weaknesses and maintain self-confidence.

Self-management refers to the ability to control impulsive feelings and behaviors, manage emotions in healthy ways, take initiative, follow through on commitments, and adapt to changing circumstances.

Social awareness encompasses the ability to understand the emotions, needs, and concerns of other people, pick up on emotional cues, feel comfortable socially, and recognize the power dynamics in a group or organization.

Relationship management involves the ability to develop and maintain good relationships, communicate clearly, inspire and influence others, work well in a team, and manage conflict.

Mindfulness Practices to Enhance Emotional Intelligence

Mindfulness Meditation: One of the most direct ways to enhance emotional intelligence through mindfulness is through regular meditation practice. Meditation helps in cultivating a deep level of self-awareness, a cornerstone of EI. As leaders develop the ability to observe their thoughts and feelings without judgment through meditation, they can better understand their internal emotional landscape and how it might influence their behavior and decisions.

Mindful Breathing: Techniques such as mindful breathing can help leaders manage stress and regulate their emotions in real-time. By focusing on their breath, leaders can anchor themselves in the present moment, reducing feelings of anxiety or overwhelm, and allowing for a more measured, thoughtful response to situations that might otherwise provoke a reactive response.

Body Scan Meditation: This form of mindfulness practice involves mentally scanning one's body for areas of tension and consciously releasing it. This technique not only promotes relaxation but also increases bodily awareness, which is often linked to emotional states. A greater awareness of physical sensations can give leaders early signals about their emotional state, providing a chance to address feelings before they escalate.

Compassionate Reflection: Developing compassion, both for oneself and others, is a critical aspect of emotional intelligence. Mindful practices that encourage leaders to reflect on their interactions with others and consider the perspectives and emotions of their colleagues can enhance empathy, a key component of social awareness.

Mindful Listening: Mindful listening is a practice where leaders fully focus on the speaker, observing their own thoughts and reactions as they arise but choosing not to act on them immediately. This practice can significantly improve relationship management skills by ensuring that colleagues feel heard and understood, thereby fostering stronger, more trusting relationships.

Applying Mindfulness to Cultivate Emotional Resilience and Responsiveness

Emotional resilience refers to the ability to bounce back from setbacks and adapt to challenging conditions. Mindfulness enhances this resilience by helping leaders maintain an emotional balance and view workplace stresses and challenges as opportunities for personal and professional growth.

Emotional responsiveness, on the other hand, involves the

appropriate and adaptive emotional reactions to various situations. By staying present and aware through mindfulness, leaders can choose responses that are proportionate and appropriate to the emotional dynamics of each situation, rather than being driven by unexamined habits or impulses.

The integration of mindfulness into daily leadership practices does not only improve a leader's capacity for emotional intelligence; it also sets a powerful example for the entire organization. When leaders demonstrate the ability to manage their emotions healthily, they inspire their teams to adopt similar practices, potentially leading to a more emotionally intelligent and mindful organizational culture.

Ultimately, the blend of emotional intelligence and mindfulness creates a robust framework for leadership that can lead to more effective management, improved leader and employee well-being, and a more adaptive and successful organization. Leaders who invest in these skills are not only preparing themselves to handle the complexities of modern leadership but are also paving the way for a more emotionally intelligent future for their organizations.

ᘖᘖᘖ

"The essence of mindful leadership is transforming challenges into opportunities for growth. This transformation is not just about business outcomes but about enriching the lives of those we lead."

ϷϷϷ

FIVE

THE ART OF MINDFUL COMMUNICATION

Effective communication is a cornerstone of successful leadership, and the integration of mindfulness into communication practices can significantly enhance the quality of interactions within an organization. Mindful communication involves being fully present and attentive during interactions, listening deeply, and speaking with intention and clarity. This approach not only fosters clearer understanding and greater connection but also helps to prevent misunderstandings and conflicts.

Principles of Mindful Communication

The essence of mindful communication lies in its capacity to strengthen the connections between people. It involves more than just the words spoken; it also encompasses how messages are delivered and received, including body language, tone of voice, and even the timing of the communication. The principles of mindful communication can be distilled into several key practices:

Listening with Full Attention: Mindful listening requires giving full attention to the speaker, without planning what to say next or judging the content. This allows for a deeper understanding of the other person's perspective and can significantly enhance the quality of interactions.

Speaking with Awareness: Mindful speaking involves being aware of the impact of one's words and choosing them wisely. It means speaking truthfully without causing harm and expressing oneself clearly and directly.

Pausing Before Responding: A mindful pause before responding gives one the time to consider the best way to communicate their thoughts and feelings. This pause can help to manage impulses that might lead to inappropriate or harmful responses, especially in high-stress situations.

Nonverbal Communication: Being mindful of nonverbal cues—such as facial expressions, gestures, and posture—is essential as these often communicate more than words. Mindful awareness of one's own nonverbal signals, as well as attentiveness to those of others, can enhance the clarity and depth of interactions.

Strategies for Improving Communication through Mindfulness

Daily Mindfulness Meditation: Regular meditation practice can improve focus and reduce reactivity. It enhances the ability to remain present during conversations, making it easier to listen deeply and respond thoughtfully.

Reflective Listening: This technique involves listening to understand, then reflecting back what is heard to confirm understanding. This not only improves clarity but also shows respect and care for the speaker's point of view, building trust and openness in relationships.

Mindful Emailing and Messaging: In the digital age, mindful communication extends to written forms. Before sending an email or message, taking a moment to read it from the recipient's perspective can prevent misunderstandings. This includes being clear and direct, using empathetic language, and considering the appropriate timing for sending messages.

Regular Check-Ins: Implementing regular check-ins with team members or colleagues can help foster open lines of communication. These meetings can be opportunities to practice mindful listening and speaking, addressing potential issues before they escalate and reinforcing a culture of mindful communication.

Conflict Resolution: Mindful communication is particularly valuable in conflict resolution. Approaching conflicts with a mindset of openness and non-judgment allows for more productive discussions and more sustainable resolutions. Acknowledging emotions without allowing them to dominate the conversation can lead to clearer understanding and mutual respect.

The Impact of Mindful Communication on Leadership

When leaders practice mindful communication, they model those skills to their teams, setting a standard for interaction that can transform organizational culture. Teams led by mindful communicators tend to experience higher levels of engagement, reduced conflict, and enhanced collaboration. Leaders themselves find that mindful communication helps them to be more persuasive and inspiring, aligning their teams more effectively towards common goals.

Furthermore, mindful communication can lead to better decision-making. By ensuring that all voices are heard and that all viewpoints are considered, leaders can avoid the pitfalls of biased or incomplete information. This inclusiveness leads to more robust decision-making processes and outcomes that are more widely supported within the organization.

The art of mindful communication is a powerful tool for leaders. It enhances the effectiveness of interactions, builds stronger relationships, and creates a more positive and productive work environment. By investing in the development of mindful communication skills, leaders can profoundly impact their personal effectiveness and the success of their organizations.

▷▷▷

"Leaders who practice mindfulness witness a profound shift in their approach to management—from reactive to reflective, from hurried to deliberate. This shift is crucial for modern management."

❧❧❧

SIX

DECISION MAKING WITH CLARITY

In the fast-paced, high-stakes environment of modern leadership, decision-making can be a formidable challenge. The ability to make clear, effective decisions is crucial for success, but the constant barrage of information and demands can cloud judgment. Meditation, as a tool of mindfulness, offers significant benefits in sharpening the decision-making process. By fostering a calm, clear state of mind, meditation helps leaders manage stress, focus on relevant information, and approach complex decisions with poise and clarity.

The Role of Meditation in Enhancing Decision-Making

Meditation helps to cultivate a heightened state of awareness and focused attention. This practice involves quieting the mind and gradually training it to reduce the influence of external distractions and internal biases. Regular meditation practice can improve cognitive functions such as attention, concentration, and emotional regulation—each of which plays a critical role in decision-making.

Reducing Stress and Anxiety: High levels of stress and anxiety can impede effective decision-making, leading to rushed or emotionally charged choices that may not result in the best outcomes. Meditation reduces stress by lowering cortisol levels in the brain and promoting a relaxed state of mind. This tranquility allows leaders to approach decisions with a balanced perspective, free from the clouding effects of stress.

Enhancing Concentration: Meditation increases the brain's ability to concentrate and maintain attention on specific tasks. This improved focus allows leaders to better analyze complex information, consider alternatives, and foresee potential consequences without becoming overwhelmed.

Increasing Emotional Intelligence: By promoting greater self-awareness and emotional control, meditation enables leaders to recognize their own emotional responses to various options and consider them judiciously in the decision-making process. This self-awareness is crucial in avoiding decisions that are overly influenced by transient emotions or biases.

Techniques of Meditation for Decision-Making

Focused Attention Meditation: This form of meditation involves concentrating on a single point of reference, such as the breath, a mantra, or a specific object. It trains the mind to focus and redirect attention when it wanders, which can be particularly beneficial in maintaining focus during complex decision-making processes.

Open Monitoring Meditation: In contrast to focused attention, open monitoring meditation involves observing all aspects of one's experience without attachment to any particular object or thought. This practice can enhance a leader's ability to absorb and process information without prejudice, an essential skill in evaluating multiple sides of an argument or scenario.

Guided Visualization: This technique involves mentally simulating various outcomes of a decision. Through guided visualization, leaders can explore potential scenarios in a controlled, mindful way, helping to identify potential risks and rewards that might not be as evident through traditional analysis.

Mindfulness Walking: Walking meditation combines physical activity with mindful awareness, which can be especially useful for leaders who find still meditation challenging. Walking in a calm and relaxed environment while gently maintaining an awareness of the body and surroundings can clear the mind and facilitate better access to intuitive knowledge and rational analysis.

Applying Meditation to Real-World Decision-Making

Routine Incorporation: To effectively enhance decision-making, meditation should be practiced regularly, not just during times of difficult decisions. Integrating meditation into the daily routine builds the mental resilience and clarity that leaders can draw upon when needed.

Pre-Decision Calm: Engaging in a short meditation session before making significant decisions can help clear the mind and reduce noise from irrelevant factors. This practice can ensure that decisions are based more on balanced reasoning and less on impulsive reactions.

Post-Decision Reflection: After a decision is made, meditation can be used to reflect on the decision process and outcomes. This helps in understanding the efficacy of the decision, learning from the experience, and improving future decision-making processes.

Team Decision-Making: Encouraging meditation practices within teams can enhance collective decision-making. Teams that meditate together may experience increased alignment and harmony, leading to more coherent and unified decision processes.

The practice of meditation offers powerful benefits for enhancing the clarity and effectiveness of decision-making in leadership. Through regular practice, leaders can develop a keener awareness and a more focused mind, enabling them to navigate the complexities of their roles with wisdom and insight. As the modern business environment continues to evolve, the integration of meditation into the decision-making process represents a forward-thinking approach to cultivating leadership capabilities that are both robust and resilient.

ᗞᗞᗞ

"Emotional intelligence in leadership is not a bonus; it's a necessity. Mindfulness sharpens this intelligence, enabling leaders to navigate the complexities of human emotions with finesse and empathy."

ᐅᐅᐅ

SEVEN

STRESS MANAGEMENT FOR LEADERS

Leadership inherently involves high-stakes decision-making, responsibility, and often, intense pressure. These demands can lead to significant stress, which if not managed properly, can impair a leader's effectiveness and well-being. Effective stress management is therefore crucial for leaders to maintain not only their own health but also to set a positive example for their teams. Implementing techniques that help manage and mitigate stress is vital for sustaining performance and fostering a healthy work environment.

Understanding Stress in Leadership

Stress is the body's response to any demand for change. In a leadership context, stressors can range from workload and performance pressures to interpersonal conflicts and organizational changes. While a moderate amount of stress can enhance performance by providing motivation and energy, excessive stress can lead to burnout, decision fatigue, and decreased productivity.

Recognizing the sources of stress and understanding its effects on the mind and body is the first step toward effective management. Symptoms of stress in leaders can manifest as irritability, difficulty making decisions, fatigue, and a decline in physical health. Awareness of these signs is crucial as it prompts the initiation of strategies to alleviate stress before it becomes overwhelming.

Techniques for Managing Stress

Regular Physical Activity: Engaging in physical exercise is one of the most effective ways to combat stress. Activities like running, swimming, or even brisk walking increase the production of endorphins, the brain's feel-good neurotransmitters. Leaders can incorporate physical activity into their routine by scheduling regular workouts, using walking meetings, or encouraging team-based sports.

Mindfulness and Meditation: Mindfulness meditation has been shown to reduce stress significantly by enhancing an individual's ability to regulate emotions. Techniques such as guided imagery, deep breathing exercises, and body scans can help leaders focus their attention away from the source of stress. Practicing these techniques regularly can cultivate a state of mind that is more resilient to stress.

Effective Time Management: Poor time management can significantly increase workplace stress. Leaders can adopt techniques such as prioritizing tasks, delegating responsibilities, and setting realistic deadlines to manage their workload better. Tools like digital planners or apps can be particularly useful in organizing tasks and reminders efficiently.

Setting Boundaries: In the digital age, work can easily spill into personal time. Leaders must set clear boundaries between work and personal life to ensure adequate downtime, which is essential for mental and physical recovery. This might mean having designated times when they are not available to respond to work-related messages or calls.

Building a Support Network: Having a robust support system can alleviate stress significantly. This can include peers, mentors, or professional counselors who can provide advice and perspective. Leaders should also encourage a culture of support within their teams, promoting open communication and mutual assistance.

Professional Development: Continuous learning and skill development can help leaders feel more competent and confident in their roles, which can reduce stress. This might involve attending workshops, seminars, or even informal learning sessions. Investing in personal and professional growth helps leaders adapt to challenges more effectively.

Integrating Stress Management Techniques into Daily Routines

The key to effective stress management is consistency. Leaders should integrate stress-reducing practices into their daily routines rather than resorting to them only in times of crisis.

Morning Routine: Starting the day with a routine that includes time for exercise, meditation, or reading can help set a calm, positive tone for the day.

Scheduled Breaks: Throughout the day, leaders should schedule short breaks to step away from their desks, practice deep breathing, or engage in brief physical activities. These breaks can help reset their mental state and reduce feelings of being overwhelmed.

Reflective Practice: At the end of the day, spending time reflecting on what went well and what could be improved can help leaders process events constructively, reducing the likelihood of dwelling on negative aspects.

Team Involvement: Leaders can also promote stress management techniques within their teams by incorporating team activities that include mindfulness practices, stress management workshops, and encouraging regular breaks.

Environment Optimization: Creating a workspace that is conducive to well-being can also play a significant role in reducing stress. This might include ensuring sufficient natural light, maintaining a clutter-free environment, and having calming elements such as plants or soothing sounds.

Effective stress management for leaders involves a combination of personal strategies and organizational practices that promote a healthy work-life balance and support mental well-being. By adopting these techniques, leaders not only enhance their own resilience but also foster a workplace environment that is more productive, harmonious, and resilient to the challenges of modern business.

ppp

"The future of leadership lies in the ability to remain present. Being fully in the moment allows leaders to forge deeper connections, spot finer details, and craft more strategic visions."

ᗊᗊᗊ

EIGHT

THE ROLE OF COMPASSION IN LEADERSHIP

Compassion in leadership is increasingly recognized as a vital attribute in creating and sustaining effective, resilient, and loyal teams. Compassionate leaders understand and care for their employees, recognizing their needs and well-being as crucial for the overall success of the organization. Cultivating compassion involves a conscious effort to develop empathy, kindness, and concern for others, as well as for oneself, which in turn enhances the workplace environment and promotes a culture of mutual respect and support.

The Importance of Compassion in Leadership

Compassion involves recognizing the emotional states of others, feeling empathy for their situations, and being motivated to help alleviate their distress. In the context of leadership, it extends beyond mere sympathy for team members' challenges; it includes a genuine commitment to acting on this understanding to support and empower employees.

The benefits of compassionate leadership are manifold. Firstly, it builds trust between leaders and their teams. When employees feel cared for on a personal level, they are more likely to trust their leaders and feel more secure in their roles. This trust is critical during times of change or uncertainty when the team's cohesion is vital for navigating challenges effectively.

Moreover, compassionate leadership can lead to higher levels of employee engagement and satisfaction. When leaders actively work to understand and address the concerns of their employees, it fosters a positive, supportive workplace atmosphere that enhances overall job satisfaction and motivation.

Furthermore, compassion in leadership encourages a more inclusive workplace. It promotes understanding and tolerance among diverse team members, which is essential in a globalized business environment where cross-cultural teams are common. Compassionate leaders are skilled at managing and valuing diversity, which enhances team creativity and problem-solving by integrating a wide range of perspectives.

Cultivating Compassion Towards Others

Active Listening: One of the most straightforward ways to cultivate compassion is through active listening. This involves fully concentrating on what is being said rather than passively hearing the message of the speaker. Active listening shows that the leader values the team members' input and cares about their perspectives, which can greatly enhance interpersonal relationships.

Empathy Exercises: Leaders can develop their capacity for empathy by engaging in exercises that encourage them to put themselves in their employees' shoes. For instance, spending a day performing the duties of a team member can provide insights into the daily challenges that employees face, fostering a deeper understanding and appreciation of their work.

Feedback with Empathy: Providing feedback is a critical aspect of leadership, and doing it compassionately can make a significant difference. This involves delivering feedback in a way that is constructive and supportive, rather than critical or dismissive. Compassionate feedback focuses on growth and development, which not only helps in correcting issues but also in building confidence and capability.

Recognizing Employee Efforts: Regularly acknowledging and rewarding employees for their hard work is a simple yet effective way to show compassion. Recognition can be as straightforward as a verbal acknowledgement in a team meeting or through more formal rewards systems. Celebrating team successes collectively can also strengthen group cohesion and morale.

Cultivating Self-Compassion

In addition to showing compassion towards others, it is equally important for leaders to cultivate compassion towards themselves. Self-compassion involves treating oneself with kindness, understanding, and forgiveness, particularly in the face of errors or failures.

Mindfulness: Mindfulness practices can enhance self-compassion by helping leaders maintain an objective perspective on their thoughts and emotions. This allows them to recognize when they are being overly critical with themselves and adjust their internal dialogue towards more supportive and constructive language.

Self-Care: Leaders should also prioritize their own well-being by engaging in regular self-care practices. This includes adequate rest, nutrition, exercise, and leisure activities that help maintain physical and mental health. Leaders who practice self-care are better equipped to handle stress and are more likely to model positive behavior for their teams.

Seeking Support: Just as leaders need to be supportive of their teams, they also need to seek support when necessary. This can involve discussing challenges with peers, mentors, or coaches who can provide guidance and reassurance.

Integrating Compassion into Organizational Culture

Ultimately, the efforts to cultivate compassion should extend beyond individual leaders to become embedded in the organization's culture. This can be achieved by incorporating compassion into core values and practices, training leaders and employees in compassionate communication and conflict resolution, and by designing policies that reflect a commitment to employee well-being.

The role of compassion in leadership is critical in today's business environment. It enhances individual and organizational performance, fosters positive workplace relationships, and contributes to a culture of trust and respect. Leaders who embrace and cultivate compassion set a powerful example, encouraging a more humane, supportive, and effective organizational environment.

ᕹᕹᕹ

"Mindfulness in leadership is about more than
keeping stress at bay; it's about cultivating a
workspace where innovation and creativity bloom
from a place of calm and focus."

▷▷▷

NINE

BUILDING MINDFUL TEAMS

Building mindful teams involves cultivating a group dynamic where mindfulness is integrated into the daily workflows and interpersonal interactions of the team. Mindfulness, the practice of maintaining a moment-by-moment awareness of our thoughts, feelings, bodily sensations, and surrounding environment, can significantly enhance team collaboration and productivity. When teams practice mindfulness, they develop a deeper level of understanding, communication, and cooperation, which are critical components for the success of any group endeavor.

The Benefits of Mindful Teams

Mindful teams experience numerous benefits that contribute to the overall effectiveness and health of the organization. These benefits include enhanced focus, improved stress management, better conflict resolution, and a greater ability to respond adaptively to challenges and changes.

Enhanced Focus and Efficiency: Mindfulness helps individuals to concentrate their attention on the present moment, which can significantly reduce the distractions that often occur in a busy work environment. This heightened focus can lead to more efficient work processes, as team members are more engaged and less prone to multitasking, which is often counterproductive.

Improved Stress Management: Mindfulness practices like meditation, deep breathing exercises, and yoga can help reduce stress levels within the team. Lower stress levels contribute to better overall health and well-being, which can reduce absenteeism and turnover rates, as well as improve energy levels and morale.

Enhanced Communication: Mindfulness enhances emotional intelligence, improving how team members interact with each other. This leads to better communication, as individuals are more aware of their own emotional states and more considerate of the emotions of others. This awareness helps prevent misunderstandings and fosters a more cooperative and harmonious work environment.

Effective Conflict Resolution: Teams that practice mindfulness are better equipped to handle internal conflicts. Mindfulness encourages a non-reactive, thoughtful approach to problems, allowing team members to address disputes with a level-headed and open-minded attitude, focusing on finding solutions rather than assigning blame.

Practices to Encourage Mindfulness in Teams

Regular Mindfulness Training: One effective way to build a mindful team is to provide regular mindfulness training, such as workshops or courses on meditation, mindful communication, and stress reduction techniques. These trainings can give team members the tools they need to incorporate mindfulness into their daily lives and work processes.

Mindful Meetings: Begin each team meeting with a minute of silence or a short guided meditation. This practice helps center the team and prepares them for the meeting by clearing their minds of distractions. It sets a focused and calm tone for the discussion that follows.

Creating Mindful Spaces: Designating a quiet space in the workplace where employees can go to practice mindfulness or simply take a few moments to recharge can be very beneficial. This space should be a technology-free zone, encouraging relaxation and reflection.

Mindfulness Challenges: Organize regular mindfulness challenges that encourage team members to engage in mindfulness practices daily. Challenges can include maintaining a daily meditation practice, taking regular mindful walks, or keeping a gratitude journal. These activities can be supported through apps or other digital tools that help track and support these habits.

Encouraging Mindful Breaks: Promote the idea of taking mindful breaks throughout the day. This can involve short walks, stretches, or simply sitting quietly away from one's desk. These breaks can help reduce fatigue and mental overload, boosting productivity and creativity.

Integrating Mindfulness into Team Dynamics

Beyond individual practices, mindfulness should be integrated into the team's standard operating procedures. This can be facilitated by encouraging an atmosphere where mindfulness principles are openly discussed and valued.

Open Communication: Foster an environment where team members feel comfortable expressing their thoughts and feelings. This openness can be facilitated by regular check-ins where each team member is encouraged to speak about their current projects and any challenges they are facing.

Feedback Loops: Establish constructive feedback loops that allow team members to give and receive feedback in a mindful manner. This should be a structured process that encourages positive reinforcement and constructive criticism, delivered in a way that is thoughtful and supportive.

Role Modeling: Leaders should model mindful behavior themselves. When team leaders practice mindfulness, they set a positive example for their team members, demonstrating the importance of these practices.

Celebrating Mindfulness Successes: Regularly acknowledge and celebrate when team members effectively use mindfulness to contribute to team goals. This recognition can motivate continued use and commitment to mindfulness practices within the team.

Building mindful teams is a strategic investment that can yield substantial returns in terms of productivity, efficiency, and employee satisfaction. By fostering a culture of mindfulness, organizations can create an environment that supports sustained high performance and well-being. Teams that are mindful are not only better equipped to handle the pressures and challenges of the modern workplace but also contribute to a more compassionate, thoughtful, and innovative organizational culture.

ppp

"Active listening, an integral component of mindful communication, involves more than hearing words—it's about understanding contexts, emotions, and underlying messages without judgment."

▷▷▷

TEN

Mindful Conflict Resolution

Conflict is an inevitable aspect of any organizational environment, where diverse personalities, goals, and perspectives frequently collide. However, how these conflicts are managed can significantly impact the workplace culture and overall productivity. Mindful conflict resolution offers a way to address disputes calmly and effectively, ensuring that conflicts lead to constructive outcomes rather than destructive ones. This approach involves being fully present, aware, and non-judgmental when dealing with conflicts, which can help all parties involved reach a resolution that is mutually beneficial.

The Fundamentals of Mindful Conflict Resolution

Mindful conflict resolution is rooted in the principles of mindfulness that emphasize awareness, focus, and calmness. Applying these principles to conflict situations helps in reducing the emotional volatility and promotes a more reasoned and empathetic engagement. The key to mindful conflict resolution is not to avoid conflict but to transform it into a productive dialogue.

Active Listening: This is the cornerstone of effective conflict resolution. It involves fully concentrating on the speaker, understanding their message, and responding thoughtfully. Active listening in a conflict situation requires setting aside one's own agenda to understand the motives, feelings, and desired outcomes of the other party.

Emotional Regulation: Managing one's emotions is crucial in conflict situations. Mindfulness techniques such as deep breathing, pausing before responding, and observing one's thoughts and emotions without judgment help maintain composure. This self-regulation prevents the escalation of conflict by avoiding impulsive reactions driven by high emotions.

Clear, Compassionate Communication: Communicating in a way that is honest and compassionate is essential for resolving conflicts mindfully. This involves expressing oneself clearly and directly while also being sensitive to the impact of one's words on others. It's about striking a balance between honesty and empathy.

Non-judgmental Stance: Approaching conflicts with a non-judgmental mindset helps in understanding the perspectives of all parties without bias. Recognizing that there can be multiple valid viewpoints in a conflict encourages a more inclusive and comprehensive exploration of possible solutions.

Strategies for Implementing Mindful Conflict Resolution

Preparation and Presence: Before addressing the conflict, take time to prepare by practicing mindfulness meditation. This preparation centers the mind and equips one to handle the situation with a heightened state of awareness and calm. During the conflict resolution process, stay present and focused, avoiding distractions and staying mentally engaged.

Use of I-statements: When discussing issues, use "I" statements rather than "You" statements. For example, say "I feel frustrated when meetings start late" instead of "You are always late to meetings". This technique helps in expressing feelings and opinions without sounding accusatory, which can escalate tensions.

Seek to Understand, Then to Be Understood: Prioritize understanding the other person's perspective before trying to get your point across. Ask open-ended questions to gather more information about their feelings and viewpoints. This not only helps in finding the root cause of the conflict but also shows respect and consideration for the other person's perspective.

Finding Common Ground: Identify areas of agreement before discussing disagreements. Highlighting common interests or goals provides a positive starting point and frames the conflict as a problem to be solved together rather than a battle to be won.

Agree on a Solution: Once all viewpoints are understood, work collaboratively to identify a solution that is acceptable to all parties. It may involve compromise or finding a creative third option that satisfies everyone's needs.

Applying Mindful Conflict Resolution in Teams

To foster an environment where mindful conflict resolution becomes the norm, it's essential to train and empower teams with these skills. Conducting regular workshops or training sessions on mindfulness and conflict resolution techniques can help embed these practices in the organizational culture.

Leaders can also model mindful conflict resolution in their interactions, demonstrating how conflicts can be handled constructively. This sets a precedent for team members, who are more likely to emulate these strategies in their own interactions.

Creating policies that support and promote mindful conflict resolution practices, such as structured mediation processes or regular check-ins, can also institutionalize these approaches within an organization.

Mindful conflict resolution is an invaluable skill set that transforms potential disruptions into opportunities for growth and development. By approaching conflicts with mindfulness, organizations can not only resolve disputes more effectively but also enhance interpersonal relationships and foster a supportive and collaborative work environment. This ultimately leads to a more harmonious, productive, and resilient organization.

ᐳᐳᐳ

"A mindful leader transforms the workplace into a realm of possibility. Each mindful practice is a step toward a more engaged, supportive, and resilient organizational culture."

ᐅᐅᐅ

ELEVEN

THE LEADER'S MEDITATION TOOLKIT

In the dynamic and often stressful world of leadership, meditation serves as a powerful tool for maintaining mental clarity, emotional stability, and overall resilience. For leaders, having a range of meditation techniques at their disposal can significantly enhance their ability to confront various challenges effectively. This "Leader's Meditation Toolkit" is designed to equip leaders with specific meditation practices tailored to meet different situational demands—whether they need to calm anxiety before a big presentation, sharpen focus for decision-making, or cultivate compassion in dealing with team issues.

Meditation Techniques for Different Leadership Challenges

Focused Attention Meditation: This form of meditation involves focusing on a single point. This could be the breath, a specific word or mantra, a silent repetition of a soothing word, or concentration on a particular object. Focused attention meditation is particularly beneficial for leaders facing tasks that require deep concentration and precision. It helps train the mind to stay engaged and present with the task at hand, reducing distractions and fostering a higher level of detail-oriented focus.

Open Monitoring Meditation: Unlike focused attention, open monitoring meditation involves observing all aspects of experience without attachment. Leaders practice becoming aware of their thoughts, feelings, and sensations without reacting to them. This form of meditation is useful for developing a greater awareness of one's environment and a better understanding of the dynamics within a team. It can enhance a leader's ability to perceive problems or conflicts in a non-reactive way, allowing for more objective and effective management decisions.

Guided Visualization: This technique involves visualizing positive outcomes, such as successfully completing a project or achieving a professional goal. Guided visualization can be a powerful motivator for leaders, helping them maintain focus on end goals and instilling a sense of calmness by preemptively experiencing success. It's particularly useful when preparing for future events that may be causing anxiety or when seeking to reinforce the confidence and motivation of oneself or one's team.

Mindfulness Meditation: Mindfulness involves staying aware and present in the moment. This practice helps leaders manage stress by reducing tendencies to react automatically to situations, allowing for more thoughtful responses. Regular mindfulness meditation can improve leaders' ability to remain adaptable and poised under pressure. Additionally, this practice enhances emotional intelligence by improving leaders' awareness of their emotions and those of others, which is crucial for effective communication and team management.

Loving-kindness Meditation (Metta): This type of meditation focuses on developing feelings of goodwill, kindness, and warmth towards others, starting with oneself and gradually extending out to colleagues, friends, and even adversaries. Loving-kindness meditation can be particularly transformative for leaders looking to foster a positive team environment and improve interpersonal relationships. It helps mitigate feelings of hostility and conflict, promoting a more collaborative and supportive workplace.

Body Scan Meditation: In this practice, attention is moved through various parts of the body to identify areas of tension and consciously relax them. This can be particularly helpful for leaders to alleviate physical stress that accumulates in the body over long hours of work. Regular practice of body scan meditation can lead to improved physical awareness and energy management, crucial for maintaining personal health and vitality.

Walking Meditation: Leaders can also practice meditation while walking, which can be a good way to integrate mindfulness into a busy schedule. Walking meditation involves focusing closely on the physical experience of walking, observing the sensation of each step and the rhythms of the body. It's especially useful for leaders who may need a break from the office but want to continue practicing mindfulness to refresh their mind and spirit.

Integrating Meditation into a Leadership Routine

To effectively incorporate these meditation techniques into a leadership routine, leaders should aim to practice regularly, ideally daily. Starting with just a few minutes each day and gradually increasing the duration can help build a sustainable practice. It is also beneficial to vary the types of meditation used, depending on the current challenges and needs.

Leaders might find it helpful to schedule specific times for meditation, such as starting the day with a focused attention meditation to enhance clarity and focus, using mindfulness or walking meditation during breaks to maintain balance throughout the day, and ending the day with loving-kindness meditation to foster positive reflections and relationships.

Moreover, promoting a culture of mindfulness within the organization can enhance the collective resilience and effectiveness of the team. Encouraging team members to engage in meditation and mindfulness practices can lead to improved productivity, creativity, and cooperation, contributing to a healthier, more harmonious workplace.

The Leader's Meditation Toolkit offers a variety of techniques that can be tailored to meet different situational demands and leadership challenges. By regularly practicing these meditations, leaders can enhance their capacity to lead with focus, compassion, and resilience, benefiting themselves and their organizations.

ᐅᐅᐅ

"Stress management through mindfulness is not just a personal relief strategy but a leadership tool. It equips leaders with the calmness required to make thoughtful, informed decisions under pressure."

ƊƊƊ

TWELVE

INTEGRATING MINDFULNESS INTO DAILY ROUTINES

Integrating mindfulness into daily routines is a strategic approach that can significantly enhance a leader's effectiveness, resilience, and overall well-being. Mindfulness, the practice of being fully present and engaged in the moment, can transform routine leadership tasks into opportunities for personal growth and improved performance. This integration involves a conscious effort to incorporate mindfulness practices throughout the day, not just during specific meditation sessions. By weaving mindfulness into everyday activities, leaders can maintain a constant state of awareness, enabling them to manage stress, enhance decision-making, and improve interactions with others.

Understanding Mindfulness in Leadership

Mindfulness in leadership involves more than just personal meditation; it includes the application of mindful practices to various aspects of leadership, such as communication, decision-making, and problem-solving. Mindful leaders are characterized by their ability to remain present and composed, even in high-pressure situations, which allows them to respond rather than react to challenges. This heightened awareness also enables leaders to better understand and manage their emotions and those of their team members, fostering a more empathetic and cohesive work environment.

Practical Ways to Integrate Mindfulness into Daily Leadership Tasks

Start the Day Mindfully: Beginning the day with a mindfulness practice can set a positive tone for the hours ahead. This might involve a few minutes of meditation, deep breathing exercises, or a mindful walking session. Starting the day in such a manner helps to clear the mind and center thoughts, enhancing focus and preparing the leader for the challenges of the day.

Mindful Listening: Mindful listening is crucial in leadership as it enhances communication and strengthens relationships. This practice involves giving full attention to the speaker without planning a response or judgment. By truly listening, leaders can understand the underlying messages being communicated, which can be critical in negotiations, resolving conflicts, and motivating team members.

Mindful Emailing and Messaging: Email and digital communications are a significant part of modern leadership. Applying mindfulness to these tasks involves being fully present when composing messages and consciously choosing words that reflect clear intent. This helps prevent misunderstandings and promotes more effective communication. It also includes taking regular breaks from digital devices to prevent overload and maintain mental clarity.

Mindful Meetings: Transform meetings by incorporating brief mindfulness exercises at the beginning, such as one minute of silence or deep breathing. This can help all participants to be more present and engaged, leading to more productive and shorter meetings. Leaders should also practice being fully present during meetings, actively listening, and encouraging participation from all attendees.

Mindful Decision-Making: Integrate mindfulness into decision-making processes by taking a moment to center oneself before making significant decisions. This can involve stepping away from the immediate pressure to clear one's mind, allowing for a more balanced assessment of the options. Mindfulness aids in reducing the noise of biases and emotions, enabling clearer, more rational thinking.

Mindful Delegation: Effective delegation is an essential skill for leaders. Mindfulness in delegation involves considering which tasks to assign to team members while being fully aware of their strengths and developmental needs. This thoughtful approach not only ensures that tasks are suitably matched but also aids in the professional growth of team members.

Cultivate a Mindful Work Environment: Leaders can cultivate a mindful work environment by encouraging practices that enhance focus and reduce stress. This might include creating quiet spaces for meditation, encouraging regular breaks, and promoting physical activities that can be done mindfully, like yoga or tai chi.

End the Day Reflectively: Conclude the day with a reflective practice, reviewing the events, what went well, and what could be improved. This not only provides valuable insights for personal and professional growth but also helps in letting go of the day's stress, transitioning into personal time more peacefully.

Benefits of Integrating Mindfulness into Leadership Routines

Integrating mindfulness into daily routines offers numerous benefits. It enhances the leader's ability to manage stress and maintain emotional equilibrium, which is contagious and can influence the entire team positively. Mindfulness also improves concentration and memory, essential for complex problem-solving and strategic planning.

Furthermore, mindful leadership promotes a healthier work culture. It reduces burnout rates, increases job satisfaction among team members, and fosters a more supportive and innovative work environment. As leaders become more attuned to the present moment, they are better equipped to notice the nuances of their interactions with others, leading to more effective and compassionate leadership.

Integrating mindfulness into daily leadership routines is not just about adding new activities to one's schedule but about transforming existing practices with a mindful approach. By adopting these practices, leaders can enhance their effectiveness, contribute to their well-being, and inspire their teams to adopt similar habits, leading to a more mindful, productive, and harmonious workplace.

ﭺﭺﭺ

"The art of mindful leadership is mastering the balance between what is and what could be. It's about leading with an open heart and a clear mind, ready to embrace the unknown."

❦❦❦

THIRTEEN

MINDFULNESS AND INNOVATION

Mindfulness, often associated with calm and focus, can also be a powerful catalyst for creativity and innovation in the workplace. The practice of mindfulness involves being present and fully engaged in the moment without judgment. This heightened state of awareness can foster an environment that nurtures new ideas and innovative solutions. For leaders and organizations seeking a competitive edge, integrating mindfulness into their strategies can enhance the creative capacities of their teams and lead to more innovative outcomes.

The Link Between Mindfulness and Innovation

Mindfulness enhances cognitive flexibility, increases openness to new ideas, and improves problem-solving abilities. When individuals practice mindfulness, they are more likely to break away from habitual thinking patterns and explore new thoughts. This cognitive flexibility is a crucial ingredient in innovation, as it allows individuals and teams to consider unconventional solutions and approach problems from unique perspectives.

Moreover, mindfulness practice can reduce the fear of failure—a significant barrier to creativity. In a mindful environment, mistakes are viewed as opportunities for learning and growth rather than reasons for criticism. This shift in perspective can create a safer space for team members to take creative risks and express their ideas without fear of negative consequences.

Strategies to Foster Creativity and Innovation Through Mindfulness

Creating Space for Mindful Reflection: Innovation often starts with reflection; a calm and focused mind is more adept at synthesizing information and recognizing patterns that may not be immediately apparent. Encouraging regular periods of mindfulness throughout the workday can provide employees with the opportunity to reflect on their projects and consider innovative solutions to problems.

Mindful Brainstorming Sessions: Traditional brainstorming sessions can often be dominated by the loudest voices, while quieter team members might not feel comfortable contributing their ideas. Conducting brainstorming sessions in a more mindful manner can help ensure that all voices are heard. Begin each session with a minute of silence to help clear the mind and focus on the task at hand. Encourage participants to respond to ideas non-judgmentally and build on each other's contributions.

Cultivating an Environment of Psychological Safety: A mindful approach to team dynamics focuses on creating a psychologically safe environment where team members feel valued and respected. This is crucial for innovation, as people are more likely to share their unique ideas when they do not fear judgment or ridicule. Leaders can foster this environment by showing appreciation for all ideas and encouraging open, empathetic communication.

Integrating Diverse Meditation Practices: Different types of meditation can stimulate various aspects of the creative process. For instance, open-monitoring meditation, which involves observing any thought or sensation without attachment, can enhance divergent thinking—a style of thinking that allows many new ideas to be generated. On the other hand, focused-attention meditation can enhance convergent thinking, the process of narrowing down those ideas to one that works.

Encouraging Mindful Walks: Walking, especially in nature, can have a rejuvenating effect on the mind and stimulate creative thinking. Encouraging employees to take mindful walks, where they focus on their surroundings and the sensations of walking, can help clear mental clutter and spark new ideas.

Mindful Listening: Innovation is not just about coming up with new ideas—it's also about building on and refining the ideas of others. Mindful listening can enhance understanding and cooperation within teams, leading to more effective collaboration and innovation. By truly listening to colleagues and considering their perspectives, team members can combine and improve upon different ideas to create something new and valuable.

Implementing Mindful Practices to Boost Innovation

Implementing these practices requires commitment from all levels of an organization, particularly from leadership. Leaders can model mindful behavior by engaging in and promoting mindfulness practices themselves. Additionally, providing training and resources that support mindfulness in the workplace can help embed these practices into the organizational culture.

Organizations might consider establishing 'innovation labs' or dedicated times and spaces where employees can practice mindfulness or engage in creative activities without the pressure of immediate deadlines. These labs can provide the tools and atmosphere conducive to mindful reflection and creativity, allowing employees to experiment with new ideas.

Moreover, integrating mindfulness into performance reviews and development plans can encourage employees to adopt and maintain these practices. Recognizing and rewarding creativity and innovation in these reviews can reinforce the value placed on these qualities.

Mindfulness can significantly enhance innovation in the workplace by improving cognitive flexibility, reducing the fear of failure, and fostering an environment conducive to creative thinking. By integrating mindful practices into daily routines, organizations can unlock the creative potential of their teams, leading to greater innovation and competitiveness in their fields.

ᐳᐳᐳ

"Sustaining mindfulness in leadership requires a commitment to ongoing practice. It's a continuous journey of growth, learning, and adapting, vital for keeping leadership skills sharp and effective."

▷▷▷

FOURTEEN

LEADING CHANGE MINDFULL

Leading change in any organization can be a daunting task, given the natural human tendency to resist the unfamiliar. However, when leaders approach change management mindfully—aware, present, and focused—they can significantly reduce resistance and anxiety among their teams. Mindfulness in the context of change leadership involves maintaining a clear, calm mind and helping others navigate the transition with a similar state of balance and acceptance.

The Importance of Mindful Leadership in Change Management

Change often stirs uncertainty and fear among employees, leading to resistance that can undermine the implementation of new strategies or processes. Mindful leadership can counteract these effects by fostering an environment of open communication and trust. When leaders are fully present and genuinely attentive, they can better understand and address the concerns and emotions of their employees, helping to ease the transition.

Additionally, mindful leadership helps in maintaining one's own equilibrium amidst the stress of change. It enables leaders to model calm and composed behavior, setting a psychological tone that encourages others to emulate these attributes. This composure is crucial during times of transition, as it helps stabilize the team and guide them through uncertainty with confidence.

Techniques for Managing Change with Mindfulness

Open Communication: One of the first steps in mindful change management is to ensure that communication is transparent and ongoing. Leaders should provide clear, concise information about what the change entails and how it will affect the team. Regular updates and open forums for discussion allow employees to feel involved and valued, reducing feelings of uncertainty and helplessness.

Empathetic Listening: Beyond just speaking, mindful leaders must also listen—truly listen—to the concerns and feedback of their team. This involves empathetic listening, where the leader fully engages with the speaker, understanding their emotional undertones and responding with sincerity. Such listening reassures employees that their views are considered, helping to alleviate anxiety and build trust.

Fostering a Sense of Control: Change can often make employees feel like they have lost control over their work environment. To counteract this, leaders can involve team members in the change process. This could mean having them contribute ideas on how to implement change effectively or asking for feedback on proposed adjustments. Giving employees a role in the process not only reduces resistance but also enhances their engagement and commitment to the new direction.

Practicing and Promoting Resilience: Change is an inevitable part of organizational growth, and cultivating resilience is key to navigating it successfully. Mindfulness practices such as meditation, deep breathing exercises, or yoga can help enhance resilience by reducing stress and improving emotional regulation. Leaders should not only practice these techniques themselves but also encourage their teams to adopt them.

Regular Mindfulness Training: Conducting workshops or training sessions that focus on mindfulness can equip employees with tools to manage their reactions to change more effectively. These sessions can cover various aspects of mindfulness practice, from basic meditation to advanced techniques for managing stress and anxiety.

Celebrating Milestones: Mindful leaders recognize the importance of acknowledging and celebrating progress. By setting and commemorating milestones, leaders can give their teams a sense of accomplishment and a moment to reflect on how far they have come. These celebrations can boost morale and motivate teams to continue embracing the new changes.

Integrating Mindfulness into the Fabric of Change

To make mindfulness a core part of change management, leaders must integrate it into the daily routines of the organization. This could involve starting meetings with a minute of silence to center the group or creating quiet spaces where employees can go to practice mindfulness during the day. Additionally, leaders should consistently demonstrate mindfulness in their behavior, showing patience, consideration, and calmness in their decision-making and interactions.

Adaptability through Mindful Observance: Being mindful also means being adaptable. Leaders should keep a close watch on how change is impacting their team, staying alert to both positive progress and signs of distress. This awareness allows them to adjust strategies as needed, demonstrating to their teams that the process is flexible and responsive to their needs.

Creating a Supportive Atmosphere: Finally, the overarching aim of mindful change leadership should be to cultivate a supportive atmosphere that endures beyond the immediate change. This involves reinforcing values of mindfulness, empathy, and resilience, making them key components of the organization's culture.

Leading change mindfully is about more than managing logistics; it's about guiding people through transformation in a way that respects their experience and leverages their strengths. By applying mindfulness to change management, leaders can not only reduce resistance and anxiety but also inspire a more adaptable, innovative, and cohesive team culture.

ᐅᐅᐅ

"By integrating mindfulness into leadership, we
don't just change the way we work; we change how
we perceive challenges, interact with others, and
ultimately, how we understand ourselves."

ﭞﭞﭞ

FIFTEEN

Mindful Leadership and Ethics

In the complex and fast-paced world of modern leadership, ethical decision-making is more crucial than ever. Mindfulness, with its emphasis on awareness, focus, and presence, can be a powerful ally in enhancing the ethical standards of leadership. By encouraging a deep connection with one's core values and a compassionate understanding of others' perspectives, mindfulness can lead to more ethical behaviors and decisions in professional settings.

The Connection Between Mindfulness and Ethical Leadership

Ethical leadership involves making decisions that are not only legally compliant but also morally sound and demonstrative of good character. Mindfulness enriches this process by fostering greater self-awareness and empathy, which are essential for understanding the broader impact of one's decisions. A mindful leader is typically more attuned to the effects of their actions on others, leading to a more considerate and ethical approach to leadership.

Increased Self-Awareness: Mindfulness meditation and practices enhance self-awareness, helping leaders become more conscious of their thoughts, emotions, and biases. This awareness is crucial for ethical decision-making, as it allows leaders to recognize when their personal biases might cloud their judgment or when they might be tempted to make decisions that benefit themselves at the expense of others.

Enhanced Empathy: Regular mindfulness practice can increase a person's capacity for empathy, making it easier to understand and consider the feelings and viewpoints of others. In leadership, this empathetic stance can prevent harmful decisions that might negatively affect stakeholders and instead promote actions that consider the well-being of all involved.

Reduced Reactivity: Mindfulness helps in managing emotional reactivity. Leaders who practice mindfulness are less likely to make impulsive decisions based on emotions such as fear, anger, or frustration, which can often lead to unethical outcomes. Instead, they can approach situations with a calm and balanced mind, ensuring that their decisions are thoughtful and considerate.

Mindful Techniques for Ethical Decision-Making

Mindful Reflection: Before making significant decisions, leaders can engage in mindful reflection. This involves taking time to contemplate the decision at hand while being fully present. During this reflection, leaders can consider the ethical implications of their choices and align their decisions with their core values and the organization's ethical standards.

Ethical Meditations: Specific meditations can be designed to focus on ethical dilemmas and moral values. For instance, leaders can meditate on scenarios where they must choose between difficult options, focusing on aligning their thoughts with ethical practices and considering the welfare of others involved.

Regular Check-ins with Core Values: Leaders can set aside regular periods for reviewing the core values that guide their professional conduct. This practice can be integrated into daily or weekly routines and can serve as a reminder of the leader's commitment to ethical behavior. These check-ins can be supported by mindfulness practices that focus on intentionality and purpose.

Stakeholder Considerations: When faced with decisions, mindful leaders can practice techniques that involve considering the perspectives of all stakeholders. This might include visualizing the impact of decisions on different groups, from employees and customers to the broader community and the environment.

Mindful Techniques for Managing Change

Transparent Communication: Mindful leadership involves open and honest communication, especially during periods of change. By clearly explaining the reasons for change and the expected outcomes, a leader can mitigate fear and uncertainty, which often lead to resistance.

Empathetic Listening Sessions: Organizing sessions where employees can express their concerns and feelings about the change can be beneficial. Leaders should practice empathetic listening during these sessions, demonstrating genuine care and consideration for the feelings of their team members.

Mindfulness-Based Stress Reduction Techniques: Introducing techniques such as guided meditations, breathing exercises, and yoga can help reduce the stress and anxiety associated with change. These practices not only support individual coping mechanisms but also foster a collective sense of calm within the team.

Cultivating Resilience and Flexibility: Regular mindfulness practice can enhance resilience, helping both leaders and their teams to adapt more readily to change. Resilient teams are less likely to experience anxiety and resistance, as they feel more capable of handling new challenges.

Integrating mindfulness into leadership not only enhances ethical decision-making but also provides effective strategies for managing organizational change. These practices help leaders navigate the complexities of their roles with integrity and consideration, ultimately promoting a more ethical, compassionate, and adaptive organizational culture. Through mindful leadership, ethics becomes not just a compliance issue but a lived value that guides all organizational activities and interactions.

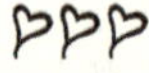

"Every mindful step in leadership is a leap towards a more empathetic, understanding, and effective management style. It's about small moments having a big impact."

❤❤❤

SIXTEEN

SUSTAINING MINDFULNESS IN LEADERSHIP

Sustaining mindfulness in leadership involves more than the occasional meditation session; it requires a commitment to continuously cultivate mindfulness throughout all aspects of leadership. This commitment helps leaders remain effective, composed, and empathetic, even in the face of the complex challenges that characterize modern organizational life. Implementing strategies that embed mindfulness into the daily routine can ensure that mindfulness becomes a foundational element of a leader's approach, fostering a work culture that values deep awareness and thoughtful response.

Integrating Mindfulness into Daily Leadership Activities

To sustain mindfulness in leadership, it is essential to integrate mindful practices into daily activities systematically. This integration helps ensure that mindfulness is not seen as just an add-on or a temporary fix but as an integral part of the leadership style.

Routine Mindfulness Practice: Establishing a routine of daily mindfulness exercises is crucial. Leaders might start their day with meditation, engage in mindful walking during lunch breaks, or practice mindfulness during transitions between meetings. Consistency is key—the more regularly mindfulness is practiced, the more it becomes second nature.

Mindful Scheduling: Leaders often have demanding schedules, so integrating mindfulness into their calendar can help maintain this practice. This could include setting aside specific times for brief mindfulness sessions throughout the day or ensuring that there are opportunities for mindful reflection before making significant decisions.

Mindfulness Reminders: Setting up reminders can help sustain mindfulness practices. Whether it's an app notification or a note in a planner, reminders can prompt leaders to take short mindfulness breaks. These pauses are vital for reconnecting with the present moment and can significantly enhance decision-making and interpersonal interactions.

Mindful Communication: Applying mindfulness to communication involves being fully present during conversations, listening actively, and responding thoughtfully. Leaders can practice this by focusing solely on the conversation at hand, avoiding distractions like smartphones or computers during interactions, which demonstrates respect and value for the speaker and enhances the quality of communication.

Training and Resources

Providing continuous learning opportunities for mindfulness can help leaders keep their practice fresh and engaging. This can involve various resources and training opportunities.

Ongoing Training and Workshops: Regular workshops or training sessions on mindfulness can provide leaders and their teams with new techniques and insights, helping to deepen their practice and understanding of mindfulness.

Mindfulness Coaching: Personal coaching on mindfulness can offer leaders tailored guidance on deepening their practice and overcoming any challenges they encounter in maintaining mindfulness in their leadership roles.

Reading and Resources: Encouraging leaders to read books, listen to podcasts, or use apps focused on mindfulness can provide ongoing inspiration and knowledge. This can help leaders stay motivated and find new ways to integrate mindfulness into their daily routines.

Creating a Supportive Environment

Leaders have a significant influence on organizational culture. By fostering an environment that supports mindfulness, leaders can encourage their teams to adopt similar practices.

Mindful Meetings: Start meetings with a minute of mindfulness or a brief guided meditation. This not only helps everyone present to center themselves but also enhances focus and productivity during the meeting.

Mindful Spaces: Creating spaces in the workplace that encourage mindfulness, such as quiet zones or meditation rooms, can support employees in developing their own practices.

Promoting Work-Life Balance: Leaders who prioritize work-life balance set a powerful example for their teams. Encouraging employees to manage their workloads mindfully and take time for personal well-being can reduce burnout and increase overall job satisfaction and productivity.

Evaluating and Adjusting Practices

To sustain mindfulness effectively, leaders should regularly evaluate their practices and make adjustments as needed. This evaluation can involve personal reflection on what aspects of mindfulness are most beneficial or feedback from colleagues and team members.

Feedback Mechanisms: Implement regular feedback sessions where team members can share how mindfulness practices are impacting their work and well-being. This feedback can provide valuable insights into how these practices can be improved or expanded.

Adaptability: Leaders should remain adaptable in how they implement mindfulness. What works well at one point may need adjustment as personal and organizational circumstances change. Being open to evolving one's mindfulness practice ensures it remains relevant and effective.

Sustaining mindfulness in leadership requires a multifaceted approach that includes daily practice, continuous learning, supportive environments, and regular evaluations. By embedding mindfulness deeply into the fabric of their leadership style, leaders not only enhance their own effectiveness but also contribute to creating a more mindful, resilient, and productive organizational culture.

ᎮᎮᎮ

"The mindful leader sees beyond tasks and deadlines to the human emotions and interactions that drive a team's success. This vision is crucial for building strong, resilient teams."

♡♡♡

SEVENTEEN

MINDFULNESS AND EMPLOYEE WELL-BEING

The role of a leader extends beyond managing tasks and ensuring productivity; it also involves fostering an environment that supports the well-being of team members. In recent years, the focus on employee well-being has intensified, with many organizations recognizing the direct link between the well-being of their employees and overall organizational success. Mindfulness, when practiced by leaders, can significantly impact the mental and physical well-being of their teams, creating a more harmonious, healthy, and productive workplace.

The Influence of Mindful Leadership on Employee Well-being

Promotion of a Stress-Reduced Environment: Leaders who practice mindfulness inherently contribute to a calmer, more composed workplace atmosphere. Mindfulness helps reduce stress levels not only for the individual practicing it but also for those around them. A leader who is calm and present during interactions tends to diffuse stress and anxiety in others, leading to a more relaxed workplace overall. This reduction in stress contributes to lower levels of employee burnout and higher levels of job satisfaction and mental health.

Enhanced Emotional Support: Mindful leaders are more attuned to the emotions of their team members. This sensitivity enables them to provide better emotional support, recognize signs of emotional distress or burnout, and address these issues proactively. By acknowledging and validating the feelings of their team members, mindful leaders can help mitigate the negative impacts of workplace stress and create a supportive environment that enhances employee well-being.

Improved Communication: Mindfulness enhances communication skills, making interactions more effective and empathetic. A mindful leader listens actively and responds thoughtfully, fostering open communication within the team. This level of attentiveness can help in resolving conflicts more amicably and in creating a more inclusive team culture where all members feel heard and valued. Effective communication is crucial for maintaining mental well-being as it helps prevent misunderstandings and the stress that often accompanies them.

Encouragement of Healthy Work-Life Balance: Mindful leaders recognize the importance of a healthy work-life balance and encourage their teams to maintain this balance. They can set an example by managing their own workloads responsibly and avoiding overworking, which signals to employees that it's acceptable and expected to take necessary breaks and disconnect after work hours. Promoting such balance helps prevent burnout and supports overall physical and mental health.

Practices That Enhance Well-being Through Mindfulness

Regular Mindfulness Training: Offering regular mindfulness training workshops can equip employees with tools to manage their stress, focus their attention, and regulate their emotions. Training can include techniques such as meditation, deep breathing exercises, and yoga, which have been shown to improve both mental and physical health.

Mindful Physical Activities: Encouraging physical activities that incorporate mindfulness, such as yoga or tai chi, can significantly benefit physical and mental health. These activities not only improve physical fitness but also incorporate mindfulness to help reduce stress and enhance overall well-being.

Creation of Mindful Spaces: Designating quiet spaces for meditation or relaxation can provide employees with a place to rejuvenate during the workday. These spaces can serve as safe havens where employees can practice mindfulness exercises or simply enjoy a few moments of quiet.

Mindfulness-Based Stress Reduction Programs: Implementing Mindfulness-Based Stress Reduction (MBSR) programs can offer structured ways for employees to reduce stress and improve their well-being. These programs are typically structured over several weeks and focus on intensive mindfulness training to help individuals better handle stress.

Feedback and Continuous Improvement: Leaders can conduct regular check-ins with their teams to gather feedback on their well-being initiatives and make adjustments as needed. These check-ins can help leaders understand the specific needs of their team members and tailor their mindfulness initiatives to better suit those needs.

The Broader Impact on Organizational Health

The benefits of mindfulness extend beyond individual employees, influencing the broader organizational culture. Teams led by mindful leaders tend to exhibit higher levels of engagement, lower turnover rates, and greater overall job satisfaction. These factors not only contribute to a more positive workplace atmosphere but also enhance the organization's performance and reputation as a desirable place to work.

The practice of mindfulness by leaders can have a profound impact on the well-being of their employees. By fostering an environment that emphasizes mindful presence, empathy, and open communication, leaders can significantly enhance the mental and physical health of their teams, leading to a more productive, harmonious, and resilient organization.

ᐅᐅᐅ

"Innovation in leadership doesn't just come from
new ideas but from a new state of mind.
Mindfulness cultivates this state, opening doors to
creative and unprecedented solutions."

ᗵᗵᗵ

EIGHTEEN

THE FUTURE OF MINDFUL LEADERSHIP

As the business landscape continues to evolve, the demand for leaders who can navigate complex challenges with clarity, compassion, and resilience only grows. Mindful leadership, which emphasizes presence, empathy, and an ethical approach, is increasingly recognized not merely as a beneficial skill but as a necessary paradigm for future leadership. The integration of mindfulness into leadership practices is poised to reshape how organizations manage their human capital, foster innovation, and adapt to changing markets.

The Rising Importance of Mindful Leadership

The future of work is marked by rapid technological advances, shifting global economic powers, and increasing workplace diversity. These changes bring about unique stresses and challenges. Mindful leadership can be the keystone in ensuring organizations not only survive but thrive in this new era by fostering environments that prioritize mental health, adaptability, and sustained productivity.

Technological Integration and Digital Mindfulness: As technology becomes even more integrated into the workplace, the potential for digital overload increases. Mindful leadership will be essential in helping employees navigate the balance between connectivity and productivity, ensuring technology serves as a tool for enhancement rather than a source of constant distraction. Leaders may incorporate practices that encourage digital mindfulness, creating policies that help employees manage their digital consumption effectively.

Globalization and Cultural Sensitivity: Global business operations require leaders who are not only aware of but also sensitive to cultural differences. Mindfulness enhances leaders' ability to be present and engaged with diverse teams, promoting a deeper understanding and appreciation of different perspectives. This cultural sensitivity will be crucial for building cohesive teams across borders and fostering an inclusive organizational culture.

Sustainability and Ethical Responsibility: There is an increasing call for businesses to operate sustainably and ethically. Mindful leaders are more likely to consider the long-term impacts of business decisions on the environment, society, and future generations. This forward-thinking approach is expected to become a fundamental aspect of strategic decision-making in organizations striving for sustainability.

Predictions for Mindful Leadership Development

Mindfulness as a Core Leadership Competency: In the future, mindfulness is likely to be recognized as a core competency in leadership development programs. Just as strategic planning and communication skills are staples of leadership training, mindfulness techniques that enhance focus, stress management, and empathetic leadership will become standard in developing effective leaders.

Integration with AI and Machine Learning: As artificial intelligence and machine learning play larger roles in business, leaders will need to balance technological insights with human intuition and ethics. Mindful leadership will be essential in navigating this balance, ensuring that while machines may optimize for efficiency, leaders must also consider ethical implications and human impacts.

Expansion of Mindfulness Programs: Corporate mindfulness programs will likely become more sophisticated and widespread. These programs will not only focus on individual practices but also on how mindfulness can be embedded in team dynamics and organizational policies. This could include routine mindfulness breaks, mindfulness training for stress reduction, and mindful communication workshops.

Research and Innovation in Mindful Practices: As interest in mindful leadership grows, so too will research on its impact. This research will likely lead to innovations in how mindfulness is practiced within organizational settings. Tailored mindfulness practices that cater to specific industry demands or company cultures could emerge, enhancing the effectiveness of these interventions.

The Evolving Role of Leaders

Leaders of the future will need to embody mindfulness not only to manage themselves but to inspire their teams. They will act as champions of mental and emotional well-being, recognizing that these are not just personal issues but are critical to the success of their organizations. Leaders will increasingly be seen as facilitators of wellness and innovation, responsible for creating environments where employees can achieve their best work.

Emphasis on Authentic Leadership: Mindfulness encourages authenticity, a quality that will become increasingly important in leaders. Employees and stakeholders are seeking leaders who are genuine in their commitment to values and transparency. This authenticity builds trust and loyalty, which are crucial in times of uncertainty.

Adaptive and Resilient Leadership Styles: The ability to adapt to changing circumstances and rebound from challenges is a hallmark of mindful leadership. As businesses continue to face rapid changes, the capacity for resilience will become more critical. Mindful leaders, with their enhanced awareness and focus, are better equipped to navigate these changes without losing sight of their goals and values.

The future of mindful leadership is one of growth and increasing relevance. As organizations face more complex challenges and the pace of change accelerates, the qualities that define mindful leadership—presence, empathy, focus, and resilience—will become essential for anyone who aspires to lead effectively. The integration of mindfulness into leadership practices is not just a trend but a profound shift in how leadership is conceptualized and enacted in the modern age.

ÞÞÞ

"Conflict resolution through mindfulness is not about suppressing disagreements but about addressing them with clarity and compassion. This approach ensures that every conflict is an opportunity for team growth."

☙☙☙

NINETEEN

MINDFUL LEADERS IN ACTION

The transformative power of mindfulness in leadership is best illustrated through real-life examples where leaders have successfully integrated mindfulness into their management styles, leading to significant positive outcomes for their teams and organizations. These case studies provide a practical view of how mindfulness can be effectively applied in various leadership contexts, showcasing its impact on communication, decision-making, conflict resolution, employee well-being, and overall organizational success.

Case Study 1: Tech Startup CEO Embraces Mindfulness

Background: The CEO of a rapidly growing tech startup recognized the high stress levels within her team as they faced the pressures of scaling up. Concerned about burnout and its potential repercussions, she decided to integrate mindfulness practices into the workplace.

Implementation: The CEO began by introducing guided meditations at the beginning of each team meeting. She also implemented weekly yoga sessions and established a quiet room where employees could practice mindfulness during breaks. To reinforce these practices, she organized workshops on mindfulness and its benefits, providing her employees with tools to manage stress and enhance focus.

Outcome: Over several months, the team reported higher levels of job satisfaction and lower stress levels. Productivity increased, and the company saw a decrease in employee turnover. The CEO noted improved decision-making processes within the team, with employees showing greater creativity and cooperation in problem-solving sessions. The organization's culture shifted towards one of greater openness and mutual support, directly attributable to the mindfulness practices embedded into their routines.

Case Study 2: Non-Profit Organization Leader Transforms Community Engagement

Background: The director of a non-profit organization dedicated to community health was facing challenges in managing diverse teams and engaging effectively with community members. The director decided to employ mindfulness techniques to improve his leadership approach.

Implementation: He started practicing mindfulness meditation personally and soon introduced mindfulness training for his staff. The training focused on developing empathy and active listening skills. The director also incorporated mindfulness moments at the start of every community meeting to foster a space of respect and attentiveness.

Outcome: The changes led to a significant improvement in team collaboration and a deeper connection with the community. The staff became more attentive to the needs of community members, leading to more effective and sustainable health programs. Additionally, the organization experienced an increase in volunteer participation and donations, driven by the heightened sense of community and trust built through mindful practices.

Case Study 3: Corporate Executive Reduces Turnover and Enhances Leadership Pipeline

Background: A corporate executive noticed a worrying trend in employee turnover and a lack of readiness among mid-level managers to step into leadership roles. Recognizing the need for a stronger leadership pipeline and a more engaging work environment, he turned to mindfulness as a solution.

Implementation: The executive introduced a structured mindfulness program that included training sessions on emotional intelligence and leadership. The program also provided access to mindfulness apps and scheduled daily mindfulness breaks. Special attention was given to training emerging leaders in mindfulness to prepare them for future roles.

Outcome: The mindfulness initiative led to a notable improvement in leadership development within the company. Emerging leaders were better equipped to handle stress and to lead their teams effectively. The company saw a significant reduction in turnover, especially among high-potential employees. Feedback from employees indicated a greater sense of well-being and a more supportive workplace culture.

Case Study 4: Hospital Administrator Improves Patient Care and Staff Collaboration

Background: A hospital administrator was concerned about the high stress levels among staff and its impact on patient care. To address this, he implemented mindfulness practices specifically tailored to the high-pressure environment of healthcare.

Implementation: Mindfulness training sessions were tailored for different departments, focusing on stress management and empathetic patient care. The administrator ensured that mindfulness practices were short and flexible enough to fit into the healthcare workers' schedules, including brief guided meditations accessible during shifts.

Outcome: The mindfulness practices led to better stress management among healthcare workers, which directly impacted patient care positively. Staff reported feeling more present and patient during interactions with patients, leading to higher patient satisfaction scores. Collaboration among the staff improved, as team members became more attentive and understanding toward each other.

These case studies demonstrate that mindful leadership can be transformative across various sectors, from tech startups and non-profits to corporate environments and healthcare settings. By fostering mindfulness, leaders can cultivate more supportive, creative, and resilient organizations. The success stories of these leaders offer valuable insights and practical examples for other leaders seeking to harness the benefits of mindfulness in their own management practices.

▷▷▷

"In the tapestry of leadership, the threads of mindfulness weave a pattern of calm, resilience, and deep understanding. These qualities are essential for leaders facing the fast-paced changes of today's world."

TWENTY
YOUR PATH TO BECOMING A MINDFUL LEADER

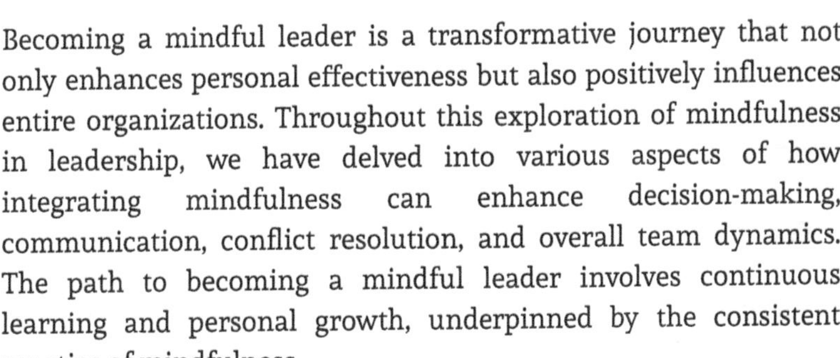

Becoming a mindful leader is a transformative journey that not only enhances personal effectiveness but also positively influences entire organizations. Throughout this exploration of mindfulness in leadership, we have delved into various aspects of how integrating mindfulness can enhance decision-making, communication, conflict resolution, and overall team dynamics. The path to becoming a mindful leader involves continuous learning and personal growth, underpinned by the consistent practice of mindfulness.

Key Takeaways from Mindful Leadership

1. Enhanced Self-Awareness and Emotional Intelligence: One of the fundamental benefits of mindfulness is the increased self-awareness and emotional intelligence it cultivates. These capabilities enable leaders to manage their emotions more effectively, understand the emotions of others, and navigate interpersonal relationships more adeptly. This emotional attunement facilitates a leadership style that is empathetic, responsive, and respectful, fostering a work environment that values collaboration and mutual respect.

2. Improved Decision-Making: Mindfulness contributes to clearer and more focused thinking, which is crucial for effective decision-making. By reducing impulsivity and enhancing concentration, mindful leaders are able to make more thoughtful and informed decisions. This capability is especially critical in today's fast-paced and complex business environment, where leaders are frequently called upon to make decisions that can have far-reaching consequences.

3. Stress Management: Leadership inherently involves high levels of stress, and mindfulness provides powerful tools for managing this stress. Techniques such as meditation, deep breathing, and mindful walking can help leaders maintain their composure even in high-pressure situations. Managing stress not only improves a leader's health and well-being but also sets a positive example for team members, promoting a healthier approach to work throughout the organization.

4. Fostering a Positive Organizational Culture: Mindful leadership significantly impacts organizational culture. Leaders who practice mindfulness and incorporate it into their leadership style tend to promote transparency, empathy, and ethical behavior. This creates a workplace where employees feel valued and understood, which enhances motivation, reduces turnover, and increases overall job satisfaction.

5. Continuous Learning and Adaptability: Mindfulness encourages a mindset of openness and curiosity, which are critical for continuous learning. A mindful leader is always learning—both from successes and failures—and is adaptable to change. This openness fosters innovation and creativity, ensuring that the organization can respond effectively to new challenges and opportunities.

Encouraging Continuous Personal Growth Through Mindfulness

Commit to Regular Practice: The benefits of mindfulness can only be fully realized through regular and consistent practice. Leaders should strive to integrate mindfulness exercises into their daily routines, whether through meditation, mindful listening, or reflective journaling.

Seek Opportunities for Learning: Mindfulness is a skill that can be deepened and enriched through ongoing education and training. Leaders can attend workshops, seminars, and courses on mindfulness to enhance their understanding and practice. Reading books and listening to podcasts on mindfulness are also excellent ways to continue growing in this area.

Cultivate Mindfulness in Others: As leaders develop their own mindfulness practices, they should also encourage their teams to adopt similar habits. By promoting mindfulness in the organization, leaders can amplify its positive effects, enhancing well-being and productivity across the team.

Reflect and Adapt: Mindfulness is not a static skill but a practice that evolves over time. Leaders should regularly reflect on their mindfulness practice and its impact on their leadership. This reflection should include feedback from peers and team members, which can provide valuable insights into how effectively mindfulness is being integrated into their leadership style.

Lead by Example: Finally, the most effective way for leaders to promote mindfulness is to lead by example. By embodying the principles of mindful leadership, leaders inspire their teams to adopt similar practices. This not only enhances the leader's effectiveness but also contributes to creating a more mindful, resilient, and compassionate organization.

The journey to becoming a mindful leader is one of continuous personal and professional development. It requires commitment, regular practice, and a willingness to continually learn and grow. By embracing mindfulness, leaders can not only improve their own lives but also make a significant positive impact on their organizations and the people they lead.

ᏘᏘᏘ

"Leading change mindfully means embracing the
flux with steadiness and grace. It's about guiding
your team through uncertainties with a confident,
calm presence that inspires trust and loyalty."

ᐯᐯᐯ

TWENTY-ONE
SUMMARY

The book offers a comprehensive exploration of how mindfulness and meditation can profoundly transform leadership practices and organizational dynamics. It addresses the modern leader's challenges and provides practical tools to foster an environment where creativity, resilience, and collaboration thrive amidst the complexities of global business landscapes.

Embracing Mindfulness in Leadership

Mindfulness in leadership moves beyond conventional management tactics to embrace emotional intelligence, self-awareness, and a compassionate approach to team interactions. The book opens with a compelling argument for the importance of integrating mindfulness into leadership roles. It suggests that leaders equipped with mindfulness skills are better positioned to make informed decisions, manage stress effectively, and cultivate a positive workplace culture.

Enhancing Decision-Making and Emotional Intelligence

One of the core themes of the book is the enhancement of decision-making through mindfulness. The practice of focused attention meditation is highlighted as a tool to improve leaders' ability to concentrate and make decisions under pressure. Open-monitoring meditation, on the other hand, is suggested for its benefits in fostering creativity and openness to new ideas, essential traits for navigating the modern business environment.

The book also delves into the significant role of emotional intelligence in leadership. Mindful practices help leaders manage their emotions and better understand the feelings of their team members. This emotional attunement is crucial for resolving conflicts amiably, providing effective feedback, and ensuring that all voices within the organization are heard and valued.

Stress Management and Building Mindful Teams

Stress management is another pivotal aspect discussed, emphasizing how mindfulness can mitigate the adverse effects of workplace stress. Techniques such as deep breathing exercises, mindful walking, and regular meditation sessions are presented as strategies to maintain mental and physical well-being.

In addition to individual benefits, the book explores how mindfulness can be leveraged to build stronger, more cohesive teams. Mindful communication practices, such as active listening and non-judgmental feedback, are recommended to enhance interpersonal dynamics and foster a collaborative team environment. The idea is to create a work culture where mindfulness is a shared practice, enhancing overall team productivity and job satisfaction.

The Impact of Mindful Leadership on Organizational Culture

The book strongly advocates for the role of mindful leadership in shaping organizational culture. Leaders who practice mindfulness set a powerful example for their teams, promoting values such as empathy, transparency, and ethical behavior. This influence helps cultivate a supportive and innovative workplace where employees feel valued and motivated.

Mindfulness and Innovation

Linking mindfulness with innovation, the book suggests that mindful practices can enhance cognitive flexibility and the capacity for innovative thinking. It posits that a mindful approach to leadership encourages an environment where creativity is nurtured, and innovative solutions are developed to meet complex challenges.

Case Studies and Real-World Applications

To illustrate the practical applications of its concepts, the book presents several case studies of leaders who have successfully integrated mindfulness into their leadership practices. These real-life examples demonstrate how different mindfulness techniques can be adapted to various organizational contexts to improve leadership effectiveness and achieve positive outcomes.

Sustaining Mindfulness in Leadership

The final chapters of the book focus on strategies for sustaining mindfulness practices within leadership roles over the long term. It stresses the importance of routine mindfulness practice and continuous learning. Leaders are encouraged to seek regular training, engage in reflective practices, and adapt their mindfulness strategies to meet evolving personal and organizational needs.

A Call to Mindful Leadership

The book concludes with a persuasive call for leaders to adopt mindfulness as a core component of their leadership strategy. It underscores that mindful leadership is not a quick fix but a profound transformation that enhances both the leader's personal well-being and the health of the organization. The narrative encourages leaders to embark on this transformative journey, promising significant benefits for themselves, their teams, and their organizations.

❦❦❦

Citation And References

This book represents the culmination of extensive research and meticulous analysis, incorporating a diverse range of sources, including numerous books, scholarly studies, and personal experiences. Additionally, I have scoured various websites to gather relevant information and data essential for the compilation of this work. I have taken every precaution to ensure the accuracy of the information presented and have diligently cited all sources to acknowledge their contributions.

Despite these efforts, the possibility of inadvertent errors remains. I deeply value the insights of my readers and appreciate any feedback that can help identify and rectify such inaccuracies. I encourage you to bring any discrepancies to my attention.

Your feedback is not only welcome but crucial, as it will aid in correcting current editions and enhancing the content of future ones. I am committed to maintaining the highest standards of accuracy and reliability in my work and thank you for your support and understanding.

Additionally, I firmly uphold the principle of freedom of speech and expression as guaranteed under Article 19(1)(a) of the Constitution of India, and I respect the diverse viewpoints and expressions of all readers.

ÞÞÞ

Other Books Of The Author

1. Empowering Minds: A Journey into Women's Self-Discovery and Power
2. The Dynamics of Motivation: Catalyzing Thought into Action
3. Meditation and Mental Well Being: The Path to Inner Peace and Clarity
4. The Psychology of Child Education: Nurturing Future Generations
5. Ethical Enlightenment: A Modern Guide to Living with Integrity
6. Voices of Empowerment: Stories of Women Rising Against Odds
7. Social Psychology in Everyday Life: Understanding Human Connections
8. The Essence of Motivational Speaking: Inspiring Change in Others
9. Balancing Acts: Women, Work, and the Will to Lead
10. Guiding with Grace: Raising Children with Compassion and Awareness
11. The Power of Positive Aging: Embracing Life After Fifty
12. Building Resilient Communities: Social Work in Action
13. The Ethical Educator: Principles for Teaching and Learning
14. From Insight to Impact: Social Psychology for a Better World
15. The Ethics of Empathy: A Guide to Ethical Living
16. The Science of Empowering the Self: Navigating Life's Challenges with Psychological Wisdom
17. The Mindful Conscious Leader: Meditation Techniques for Modern Management
18. Pioneering Spirit: Women's Pathways to Leadership and Empowerment
19. Feeling to Healing: The Role of Emotional Intelligence in Child Development
20. Transformative Talks and Words of Inspiration: Insights into Motivational Oratory

ppp

Contact

Dr. Minakshi Bansal
Social Activist
Ahmedabad, Gujarat, Bharat
minakshiindiag20@yahoo.com

❧❧❧

|| LOKAHA SAMASTHAHA SUKHINO BHAVANTU ||

● 131 ●